Art as Meditation
Harnessing Creativity for Inner Peace and Mindfulness

By
Miguel Angel Torres Vega

TABLE OF CONTENTS

1 PREFACE

1.1 Adapting Practices 4

1.2 Why Drawing 5

1.3 Personal Touch 5

2 ART AS MEDITATION

2.1 Unleashing Creativity 7

2.2 The Grounding Device 8

2.3 The Power of Presence 8

3 SET YOUR INTENTION

3.1 Purpose and Focus 10

3.2 Managing Expectations 10

3.3 Returning to Intention 11

4 CREATE A RITUAL

4.1 Preparing Your Space 13

4.2 Choosing Your Subject 13

4.3 Setting Up Tools 14

4.4 Sensory Engagement 14

4.5 Lighting and Ambiance 15

4.6 Background Noise 16

4.7 Physical Preparation 17

5 NOTICE EVERYTHING

5.1 Zooming In and Out 18

5.2 Color and Detail 18

5.3 Mindfulness in Practice 20

6 DISASSOCIATE

6.1 Breaking Labels 21

6.2 Fresh Eyes 22

6.3 Deeper Connection 22

7 FLOW STATE

7.1 Recognizing Flow 24

7.2 Achieving Flow 24

7.3 Maintaining Flow 25

8 DISCONNECT

8.1 Creating Boundaries 27

8.2 Technology Management 27

8.3 Validation-Free Practice 28

8.4 Non-Judgmental Creating 28

9 PARTING MESSAGE

9.1 Expanding Horizons 30

9.2 Embrace the Journey 30

9.3 Continued Growth 31

1

PREFACE

1.1 Adapting Practices:

Expanding Your Creative Horizons

In this guide, I will focus on drawing as our primary practice to ground us in meditation. However, it's important to note that the principles and techniques discussed here can be easily adapted to other creative practices such as painting, sculpting, collaging, creating music, or any form of artistic expression you prefer. Each medium can lend its own particular aspects to focus on. For example, in painting, one might choose to focus on color, the stroke of the brush, or the feeling of the fluidity of the paint as it glides across the canvas. In sculpture, one might focus on the sensation of physically touching wet clay, or the feeling of stacking clumps on top of one another while your wet fingers slowly form shape and volume. This is why you should not be careless in your choice of medium, as each has its own particular qualities. Drawing is the medium I am most familiar with, so it will be the focal point of our discussion. Feel free to substitute it with your chosen creative practice to suit your personal journey.

1.2 Why Drawing?:

The Benefits of a Familiar Medium

Drawing has always been my chosen medium. Its simplicity allows for an immediate connection with the creative process, requiring only basic tools like paper and a pencil. This accessibility makes it an ideal starting point for anyone looking to integrate art into their meditation practice. Drawing offers a direct path to mindfulness, enabling you to explore the nuances of your inner world through the tactile and visual experience of creating art.

1.3 Personal Touch:

Discovering the Power of Art as Meditation

I was introduced to meditation at a particularly difficult time in my life. I had a hard time dealing with my emotions, which were largely triggered by my runaway thoughts and rumination. I was instructed on a particular form of breathing and mindfulness meditation that stemmed from Buddhist monks in Tibet. Through much dedication and practice, I found many aspects of my life improving. I had increased focus, more patience, a better ability to manage my emotions, and deeper compassion. In one meditation session, I reached a flow state where my body completely took over and my breathing was in sync with the blood pulsing in my veins. I had gotten to a point in that moment that I felt as if I could control the speed of my pulse and heart by adjusting my breathing. It felt otherworldly. To describe breathing as pleasurable would do it no justice. It was as if I found the key to life. Reflecting on it, the only thing I was able to compare it to was when I would reach a flow state during hours-long life drawing sessions in college. The sensation wasn't exactly the same but very similar. Similar enough that I believed there to be a commonality underlying both experiences. Since that time, whenever I dedicated time to drawing, I would take notice of achieving this flow state, what led to it, and what effects it had on me. In each instance, as with the meditation session, I realized I achieved a point of being completely in the present moment.

2

ART AS MEDITATION

2.1 Unleashing Creativity:

The Freedom to Experiment

I challenge you to create a work that you will not share, that you will not judge, and with which you will feel the full freedom to experiment. Be present with your creation, allowing no outside conventions to interfere. This practice is for the pure experience of expression and creation—the act, the spirit, and the process. It is an exercise in setting yourself free while also mastering your inner self. We so often create art in the context of others' eyes that it can cloud the purity of the act of creation. This practice of art as meditation is a personal exercise for self-fulfillment and growth. Would you do push-ups and sit-ups in front of an audience and then ask for their immediate feedback about how you feel? It doesn't make much sense when you put it in that context. Therefore, keep your practice close to your heart and deeply personal.

2.2 The Grounding Device:

Drawing as Your Anchor

In many forms of meditation across cultures, a singular focal point is often used. This might be a set of prayer beads, a mantra, or, as in the Tibetan mindfulness meditation I have practiced, simply the breath. In our practice, drawing will serve as this focal point.

2.3 The Power of Presence:

Engaging Fully with Your Art

Drawing will be our grounding device. In the movie "Inception", starring Leonardo DiCaprio, characters navigate through different dreams that are sometimes indistinguishable from reality. They use a physical object, a "token," to remind them that they are in a dream and to break free from their mind's wanderings, returning to reality. Similarly, drawing will be our "token" that pulls us from the distractions of our minds and the noise that infiltrates our daily thinking.

Observational art, by its nature, has a built-in grounding source that keeps you engaged in the present moment. As artists, we are fortunate to have this aspect as part of our practice, whereas others may need to spend time searching for such a grounding tool. The act of drawing requires focus, attention to detail, and a deep engagement with the subject, all of which anchor us in the here and now.

3

SET YOUR INTENTION

3.1 Purpose and Focus:

Defining Your Creative Goals

What is your purpose for engaging in this practice? Do you wish to express emotion, increase skill, escape stress, connect with a higher power, or connect with yourself? Defining your intention helps to guide your practice and provides clarity and direction. Examples of intentions may be "to improve focus," or "to connect with nature" if you are drawing outdoors.

3.2 Managing Expectations:

Balancing Ambition and Acceptance

When I approach these moments, I often remind myself to be appreciative of simply having the time to create and draw, regardless of the outcome. This mindset isn't always easy to maintain, as my mind frequently bombards me with self-imposed pressures. Questions arise: Will it be wasted time if I don't like the end result? Will this drawing enhance my portfolio? Will it impact my brand as an artist if it doesn't match the quality of my previous well-received work? Does this fit with my other creations?

Recognize these thoughts as natural but let them pass. They are not the focus of this practice. Instead, focus on the joy of creating and the peace it brings.

3.3 Returning to Intention:

Staying Grounded in Your Practice

This struggle requires constant and active self-regulation. It won't happen passively, which is why setting your intention early is crucial. Your intention will serve as a focal point to return to when critical thoughts creep back in. Remind yourself of your intention: "This practice is for relaxation," "This practice is for freedom," "This practice is for expression," "This practice is for me."

Whatever your chosen intention is, ensure it doesn't impose undue pressure on you. Otherwise, you risk creating a cage for yourself from the start. There will be time for mastery, for increasing skill, for engaging with and presenting to others. Let those pursuits have their own dedicated time.

Do not let them seep into the moments you've set aside for your art meditation practice. Write down your intention and keep it nearby as a gentle reminder throughout your session.

4

CREATE A RITUAL

4.1 Preparing Your Space:

Crafting a Serene Environment

My creative spaces are often chaotic and messy, so I need to tidy up beforehand to hit the reset button and create a sense of peace and serenity. Anything that poses as a distraction from my purpose is removed, while objects and items that inspire and bring peace are allowed to stay. This preparation transforms your space into a sanctuary for creativity and mindfulness.

4.2 Choosing Your Subject:

Finding Peace in Your Art

Choosing something to draw that adds to my peace is crucial. Although I view drawing as a breakdown of shapes and values, I am careful not to select something that will frustrate me and make it challenging to immerse myself in. I might pick an object with curves and flows, making it feel like I'm riding along as I draw them. This approach transforms drawing into an adventure, an engagement rather than mere replication. It might be something as simple as drapery or cloth, or perhaps a face. Whatever you choose, ensure it is either neutral or positively associated with you, and avoid anything negative.

4.3 Setting Up Tools:

Creating a Comfortable Workspace

I enjoy setting up my tools. Despite having an abundance of art materials, there are always a few that I gravitate towards for reasons unknown. Your intention may influence whether you choose familiar tools for comfort or new materials for exploration. The journey differs when working with well-known materials versus experimenting with new ones.

4.4 Sensory Engagement:

Immersing in the Artistic Process

Regardless, when setting up your materials, ensure all of them are accessible. During our art meditation, we don't want to be distracted by searching for a tool or material needed at the moment. Having everything prepared allows us to maintain our meditation or easily return to it when our focus is broken.

For me, the ritual involves lining up my sticks of white charcoal, charcoal, and pencils, along with sharpeners and brushes. I order them, sharpen them, and ensure I feel good about them before starting. This process, though difficult to quantify, carries a spiritual nature. It's about being fully present with your tools and taking in all the sensory input. Don't rush this. Don't do it passively. Be aware of the sounds as you sharpen, the vibrations of the pencil wood scraping against the sharpener, the grit of sandpaper against charcoal. Listen to the soft, scratchy noises, smell the wood and smoky dust. You can almost create a rhythm for yourself as you go through these steps. Let it be unrushed and pleasurable, adding to the overall experience. The drawing will come, but focus on being with this moment.

4.5 Lighting and Ambiance:

Enhancing Your Creative Mood

Choose your lighting to enhance the mood and intention. Do you prefer bright, colorful, and energetic lighting, or the dimness of an old library for a mystic practice? Whatever you prefer, set your space accordingly. Consider the type of lighting—warm or cool, intensity, incandescent or LED. Pay attention to how your body responds to these elements, as they can significantly impact your meditation without you realizing it. Personally, I find bright LED bulbs too intense and their coolness off-putting, so I opt for a warm glow.

4.6 Background Noise:

Selecting the Right Soundtrack

If you choose to have music or video as background noise, ensure it enhances rather than distracts from the experience. As a musician, I avoid playing anything that might inspire me to interrupt my meditation and create something else. Instead, I play familiar albums or movies I've seen many times. If you can create without such background noise, I encourage it, as it adds another layer of presence in your drawing meditation. However, for me, having a bit of "traveling music," like John Coltrane's "A Love Supreme", enhances the experience. While it may feel like riding off another artist's moment of meditation, it's entirely okay, as this practice is about relaxation and presence.

4.7 Physical Preparation:

Nourishing Your Body for Creativity

Finally, ensure you are physically prepared. Have you eaten? Are you hydrated? Sometimes these meditative drawing sessions can last for hours. I choose to eat beforehand, but nothing too heavy that might make me sleepy. Energetic snacks like fruit, nuts, and tea keep the stomach and mind clear. I often bring tea or coffee and snacks into the studio so I don't have to disengage if I get thirsty or hungry. Imagining myself as an old artisan in a smoky studio, an earthy tea adds to this ambiance, keeping me engaged in the drawing.

5

NOTICE EVERYTHING

5.1 Zooming In and Out:

Shifting Perspectives in Observation

When engaging with your subject, imagine yourself as an ant crawling on its surface. Trace its shapes, feel its textures, and navigate each divot and relief as if they are large obstacles on the terrain you are traveling. Simultaneously, be able to zoom out and view your subject in its entirety. Observe the broad areas of surface and shapes created by the lighting. Notice the directions and turns these shapes and values take and how they relate to each other. Continuously shift your focus between the minutiae and the whole, feeling the totality of your subject.

5.2 Color and Detail:

Discovering Hidden Complexities

When I used to draw nude figures in college using color pastels, I would often focus intensely on one area of lighting on a surface of skin. From a distance, what appeared as a simple yellow spotlight on the side of a face would, upon closer inspection, reveal a complex medley of warm and cool colors dancing together. The visual mixing of these colors from a distance created the appearance of yellow, but the underlying reality was much more intricate.

5.3 Mindfulness in Practice:

Cultivating Deep Focus

I want you to approach your subject in the same way. Lean deeper in. Whether it's color, value, texture, or detail, allow your eye to explore further. You will uncover hidden complexities, but only if you spend a significant, patient amount of time with your subject. This is why it is so crucial that this practice is unrushed and uninterrupted.

This deep focus is a common element in many forms of meditation and is one of the many benefits of this practice. Your ability to focus deeply, notice more, and sustain your attention will improve with increased practice time. In the book and corresponding movie "The Peaceful Warrior", starring Nick Nolte, there is a scene where the student experiences a moment of mindfulness, noticing all sorts of small details around him, such as the movements of animals. This practice is similar. How often have you ignored the singing of birds in the morning or missed the sensation of the wind on your skin? I often practice mindfulness by following a bird in flight for as long as possible. Whenever I feel the urge to look away out of boredom or restlessness, I force myself to stay with it. This is the same approach you should take with your drawing subject. Stay with it for as long as you can. Fight the urge to look away. Look deeper. Watch what is normally unnoticed unfold before you, revealing new and unending landscapes.

As you move your hand along with these observations while drawing, don't try to capture them. Instead, ride along with them. Feel them as you travel across the page, allowing the process to be an exploration rather than a replication.

6

DISASSOCIATE

6.1 Breaking Labels:

Seeing Beyond Preconceptions

With all this emphasis on being mindful and staying with the subject, what I'm about to say may seem contradictory. It is essential to disassociate from your subject in order to truly delve deep into it. What does this mean? Throughout our lives, we have been programmed and taught to make associations for nearly everything. When you are a baby, you learn that the person who cares for you and gives you love is called "mom." This label makes communication easy, but does the word "mom" fully encapsulate all that this being is and the complete experience of it? Absolutely not. This applies to almost everything in life. We create labels to communicate our experiences easily, but the actual meaning and experience are much more complex. In our drawing as meditation practice, we aim to delve deeper into this complexity.

6.2 Fresh Eyes:

Approaching Your Subject Anew

Let's take a still life as an example. Suppose you are drawing a glass bottle with a flower in it. You must forget that it is a "glass bottle" or that it contains a "flower." Look at it without labeling or bringing any preconceived associations. Labels prevent you from fully experiencing it. Instead, delve into the uniqueness of the object's surface. Observe how it reacts with light as if seeing it for the first time. Marvel at its shape, color, and presence. Notice how it interacts with the other object—the colorful rounded shapes emerging from a round shape in the middle. Appreciate all its textures and how its parts, though thin, have real weight as they lean inside the hollow object.

6.3 Deeper Connection:

Enhancing Your Observation Skills

You must dissociate. If you are drawing a portrait, forget that it is a person. Forget the concepts of an eye or a mouth. Observe it for what it is. Do not label; only observe and create marks incidentally as you journey across its surface. Labels are constructs of the mind. The moment you name something, you are no longer in the present moment. Instead, you are in your mind, trying to make sense of it, and thus, not fully experiencing it. Stay with the experience. One can zoom in on a particular part of the subject and choose to make that the entirety of their observation, thus forcing the dissociation.

This was the essence of Dadaist Marcel Duchamp's works, in which he played with the associations we gave to objects. This is exemplified in one of his more famous works, where he labeled a toilet as a water fountain. This gesture boldly revealed the absurdity in labels and the associations we make with them.

To achieve this level of disassociation, approach your subject with fresh eyes. Engage with the object without preconceived notions. Allow yourself to be surprised by the details and intricacies you uncover. This practice will deepen your observation skills and help you connect more profoundly with your subject, enhancing your meditation and creative expression.

7

FLOW STATE

7.1 Recognizing Flow:

Identifying the Signs

You may not recognize when you are in a flow state until after it has been broken. A flow state occurs when you are so engaged in what you are doing that it has a certain level of automaticity. You are no longer steering or controlling the process; it is happening on its own. This is often likened to how someone can drive home and completely forget the journey because they were on a sort of mental autopilot the entire time. It is not that they were disconnected from the activity but rather that it came so naturally they didn't even have to think about it.

7.2 Achieving Flow:

Leaning Into Your Practice

I have often reached this state while drawing. It usually happens during the active part of the practice, not during the setup, but once I start drawing and delving deeper into my subject. The pencil is scratching, the music is playing,

I'm enjoying the ride of observing. I become one with the subject, fully in the moment, to the point of being unaware of my own presence. In my opinion, this is the peak moment of meditation. I have also experienced this in breathing meditation, where I no longer had to be consciously aware of maintaining the correct process. Instead, the process was fully internalized, and it was entirely an experience. This state, whether you call it nirvana, flow state, or something else, is ultimately where deep and dedicated practice leads.

One example of an artist achieving a flow state is in the Disney/Pixar movie "Soul." In this story, the main character, who is a jazz musician, is shown experiencing a vivid example of flow state when he veers off into a piano solo during an audition for a band.

7.3 Maintaining Flow:
Returning to the Zone

Do not feel defeated if this does not happen immediately. It takes repetition and dedication to realize these moments. The struggle comes when you achieve this state and your attention is broken. The immediate impulse is to chase it again. However, the flow state does not come by force. It occurs naturally as you lean into your practice. The proper response is to acknowledge that the moment has been broken without dwelling on it. Be aware of it and return to the practice that led you there. Return to observing, to leaning deeper into your subject, to feeling it. Eventually, without realizing it, you will re-enter the flow state. And if you don't, that's okay too. You must make space for this possibility and not view the experience as a loss if it doesn't happen. This mindset prevents you from straying from your set intention and becoming a slave to the mind and its distractions. I encourage readers to journal and reflect on what flow state was like for them, what were the elements that were present that allowed them to reach it. This is important because if you repeat and ritualize the process, it may lead to getting back to the flow state more consistently.

8

DISCONNECT

8.1 Creating Boundaries:

Minimizing Distractions

We do not exist in a world of ideals, but ideally, you would engage in this drawing meditation practice in an uninterrupted environment, free from distractions. As a father, I know this can be challenging, but it's essential not to force a session into a situation where you will be frustrated.

8.2 Technology Management:

Keeping Your Focus

This practice will not happen passively. You must make time for it. If it is a priority, you must dedicate both time and space to it. Tune out the noise. Turn off your phone to eliminate distractions. Do not open social media or document the session. Resist the temptation to video, photograph, or share the results. Put your phone on airplane mode if possible. Think of all the likely triggers that could draw your attention elsewhere and eliminate these distractions before starting.

8.3 Validation-Free Practice:
Drawing for Its Own Sake

Whenever I engage in a drawing meditation session, the results are often favorable to me. Ironically, this can defeat the purpose. My mind starts to seek validation: "Oh look, this one came out cool. Let me take a picture. Let me post it. Let me come up with a fitting caption. Let me share this tiny success." This behavior thrusts me back into my mind, seeking approval. When your drawing is done, be done with it, at least immediately. Put it away and move on to your next activity. You can return to it another time to formulate your thoughts and opinions. But for the drawing meditation, maintain the purity and integrity of the practice for its own sake. Draw for the sake of drawing.

8.4 Non-Judgmental Creating:
Embracing the Experience

Do not judge what you are doing as you are doing it. As artists, we are often our own worst critics, trained to critique and give constructive criticism. However, in this practice, we are not trying to construct anything. We are participating in an experience. Eliminate the thinking that leads you to judge your work as good or bad, as this pollutes the practice. Stay in the moment, place your mind with your subject and the action of creating. Do not lead; rather, follow where the path unfolds.

9

PARTING MESSAGE

9.1 Expanding Horizons:

Applying Principles to All Art Forms

I hope that this guide enhances your art-making experience and adds something meaningful to your practice. Remember, the steps in this guide can be applied to many activities beyond what is typically considered art, because art is in everything. Whether you are drawing, painting, sculpting, or engaging in any creative endeavor, the principles of mindfulness, presence, and intentionality can enrich your experience and deepen your connection to your work.

9.2 Embrace the Journey:

Finding Joy in the Process

Embrace the process, stay present, and allow your practice to be a source of peace, expression, and discovery. May your journey in art meditation bring you joy, clarity, and a profound sense of fulfillment. Remember, the journey itself is as important as the destination. Each stroke of the pencil, each moment of observation, and each breath you take during your practice is a step toward greater mindfulness and self-awareness.

9.3 Continued Growth:

Encouraging Further Exploration

Explore, experiment, and expand your horizons. The principles shared in this guide are just the beginning of your journey toward integrating creativity and mindfulness. Continue to discover new ways to blend art and meditation, enriching both your practice and your life. Seek out new techniques, materials, and inspirations. Join communities of like-minded individuals who share your passion for art and mindfulness. Attend workshops, read books, and engage in discussions to keep your practice vibrant and evolving.

I encourage readers to reach out to me via my website and social media so that we can share each other's experiences as they put this guide into practice. Books that have inspired me on this path are "Turning the Mind into an Ally" by Sakyong Mipham, "The Creative Act" by Rick Rubin, "The Power of Now" by Eckhart Tolle, and "The Alchemist" by Paulo Coelho.

www.ingramcontent.com/pod-product-compliance
Lightning Source LLC
Chambersburg PA
CBHW072056230526
45479CB00010B/1110